# Where's Whaley?

Written and illustrated
by Wendy Jacobs

Copyright © Wendy Jacobs

All Rights Reserved

ISBN Number 979-8-218-36604-9

For my children, who inspire me.

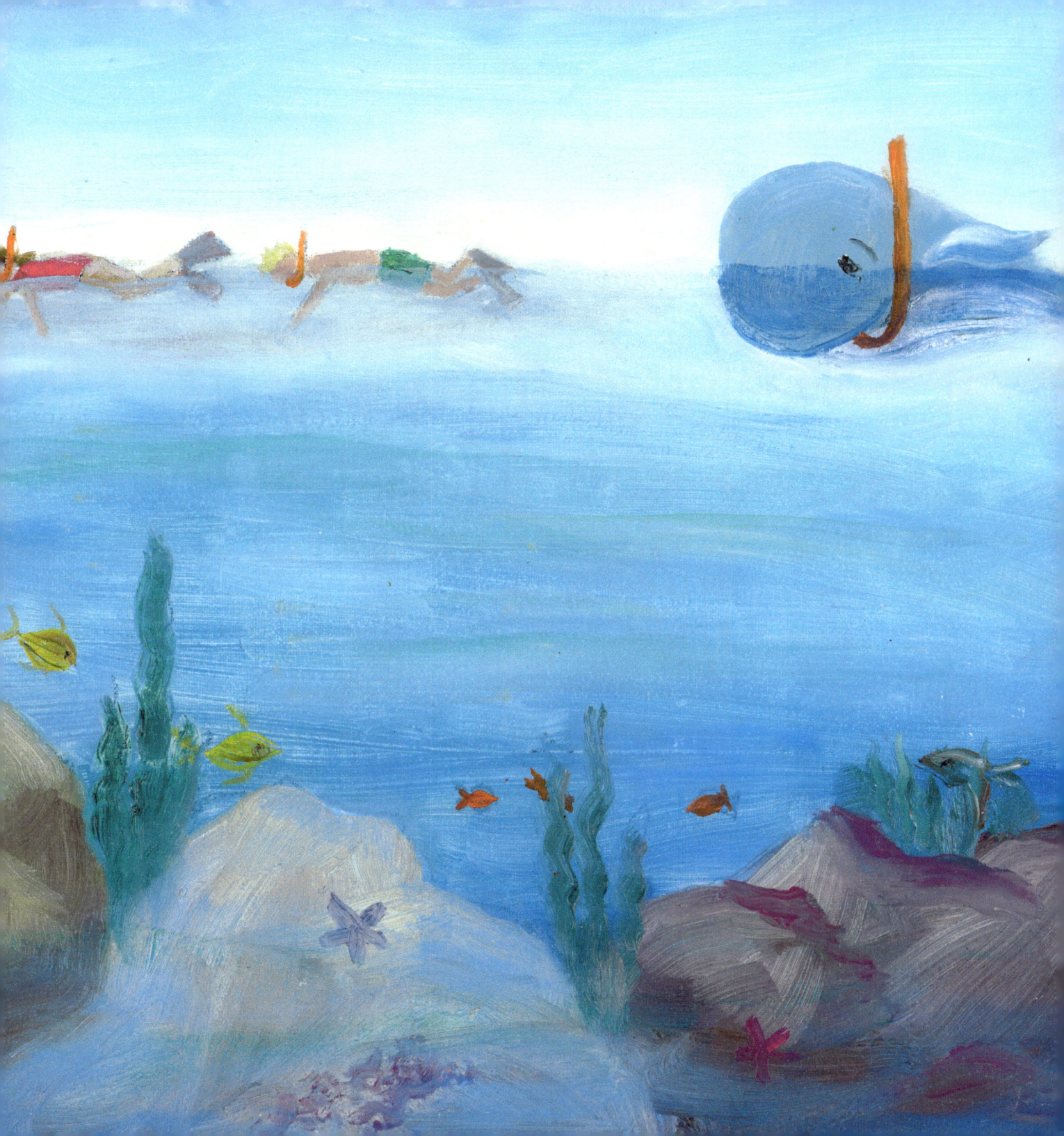

Whales are fun to watch!
They breach and flap their fins.

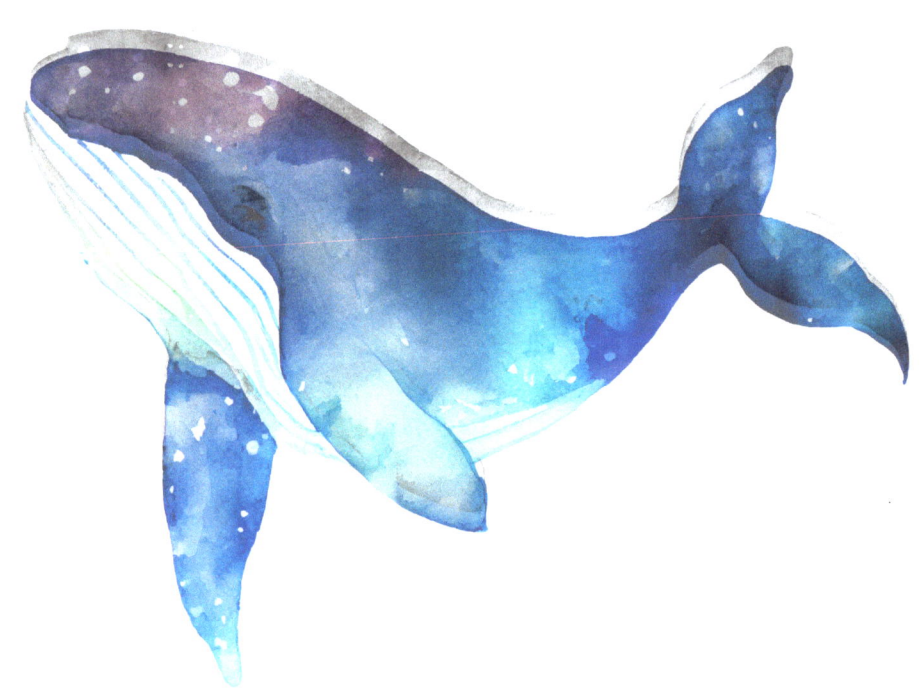

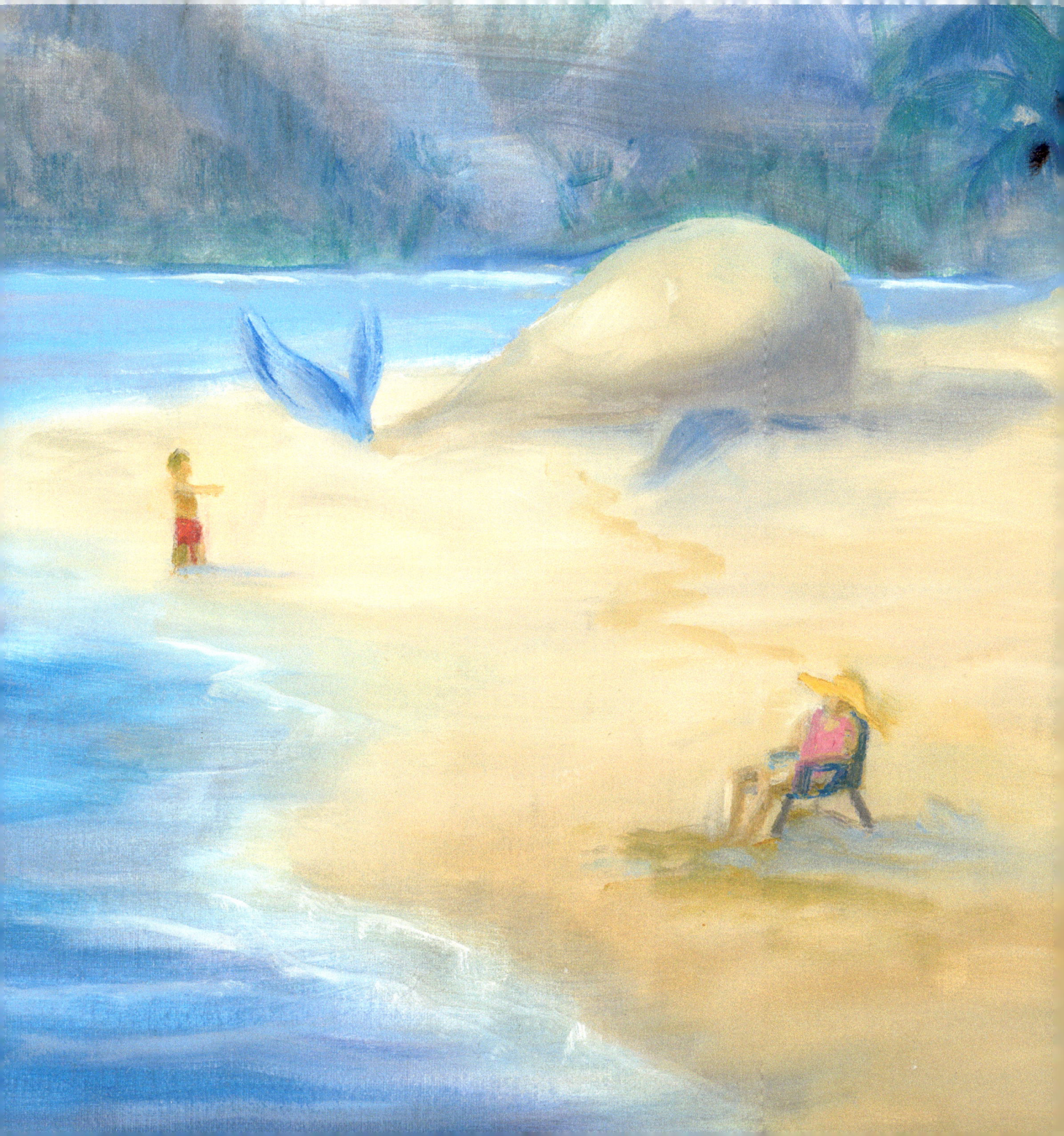

But when I play in the ocean,
I can't see them swim.

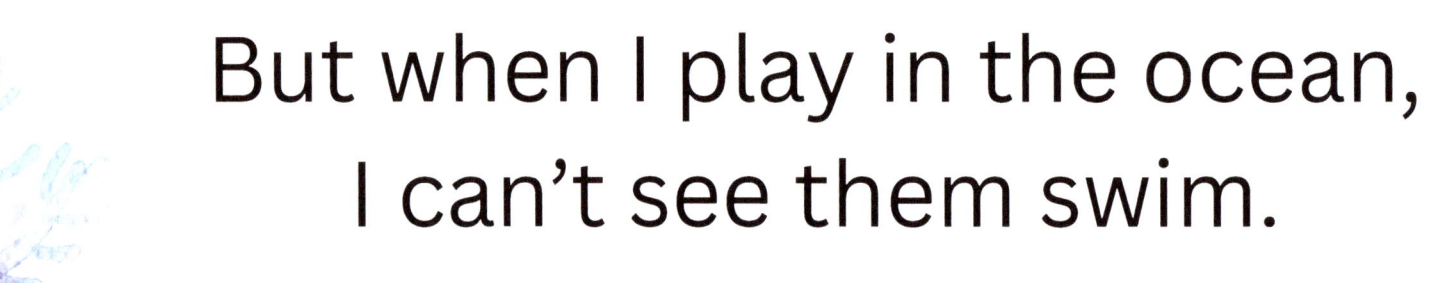

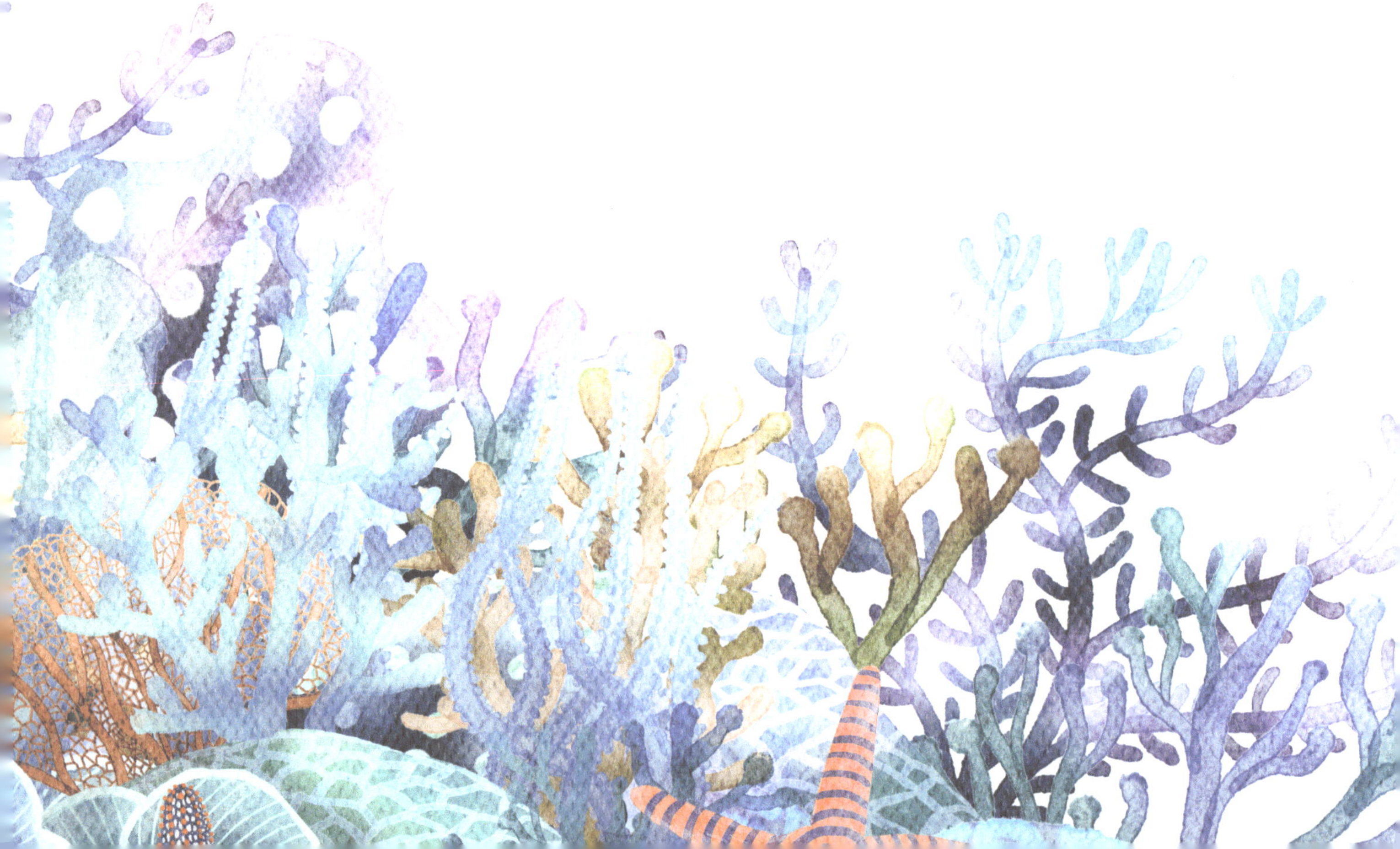

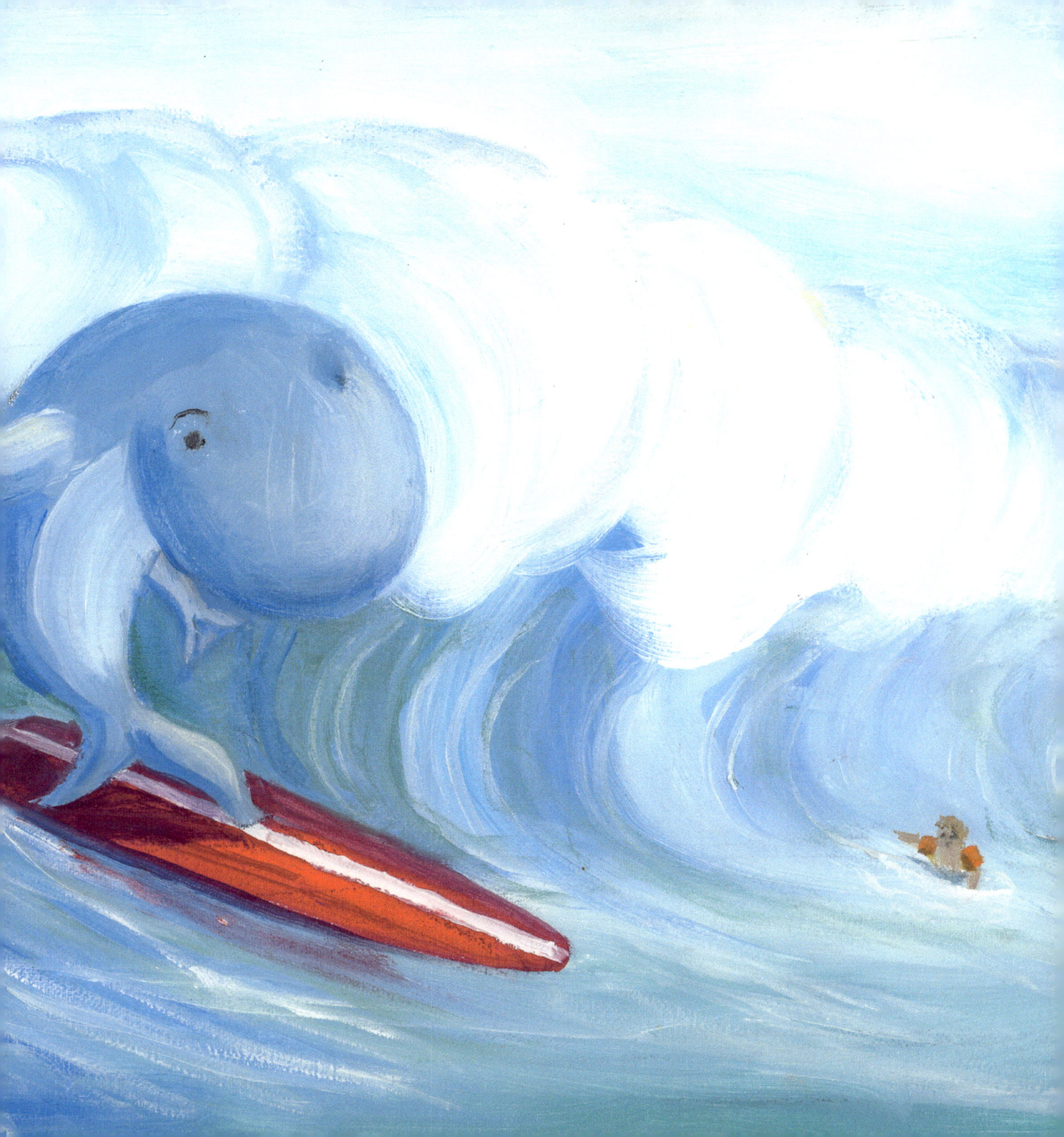

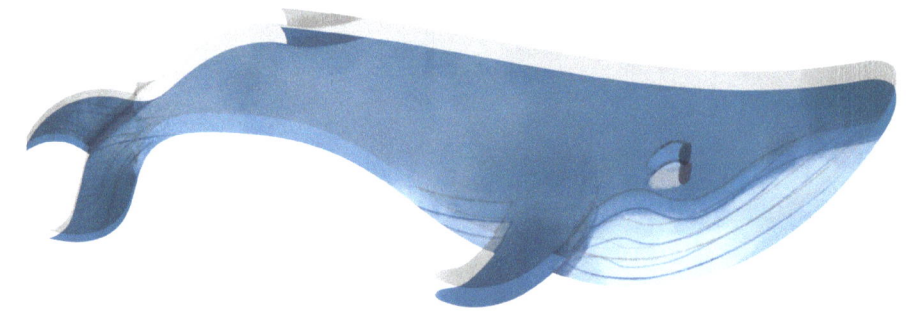

A humpback whale can grow and grow
To 40 tons and 60 feet long
So why can I not find them
When I clearly hear their song?

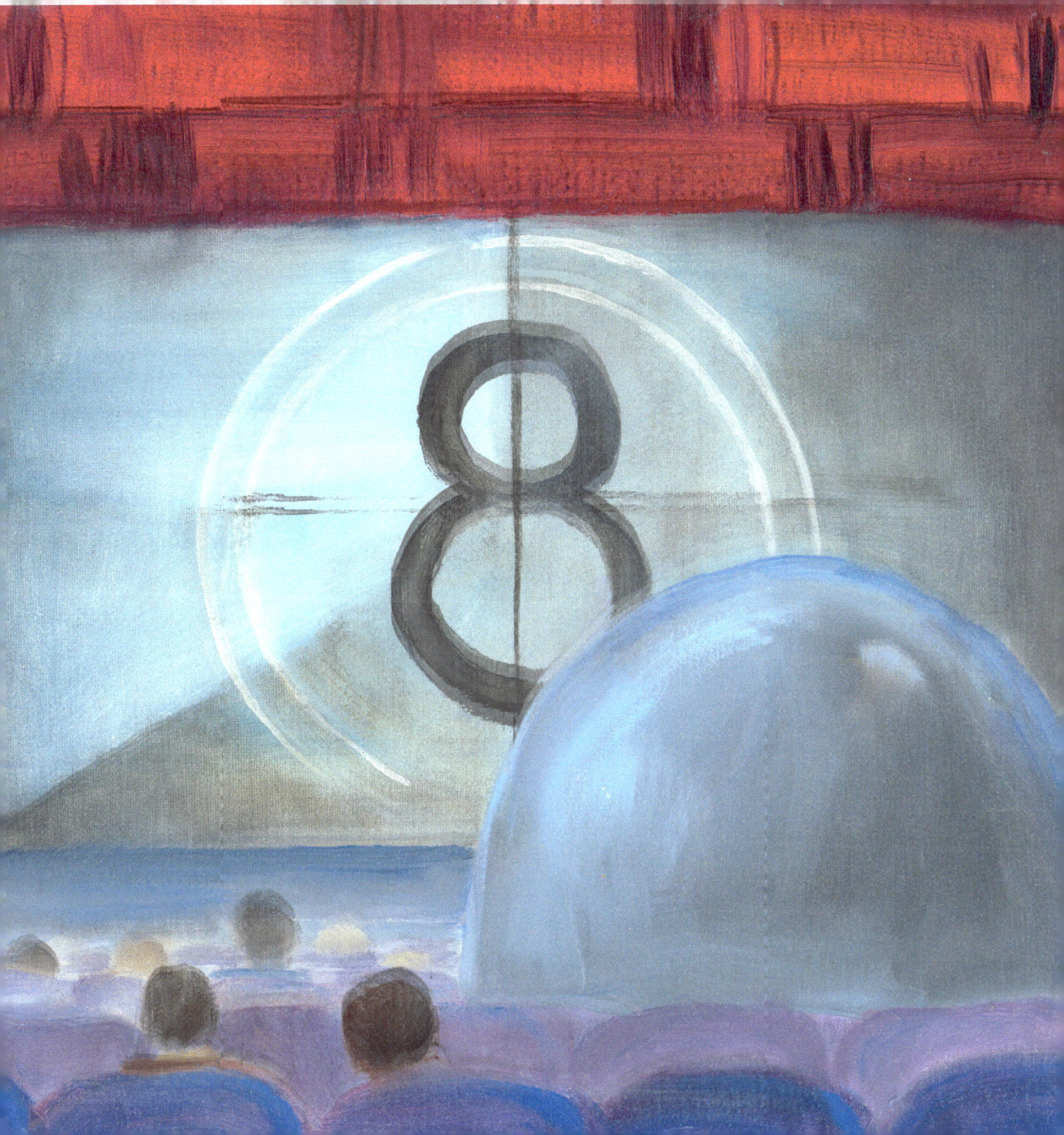

Whalesong is beautiful and each one
has a sound.
The bull, the cow, and little calf,
Up to 500 miles away can be found.

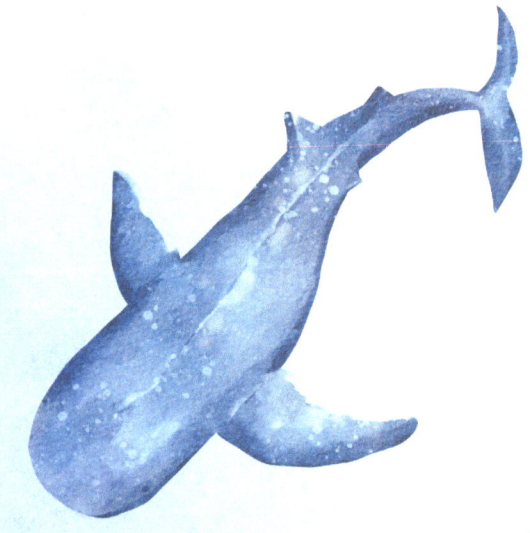

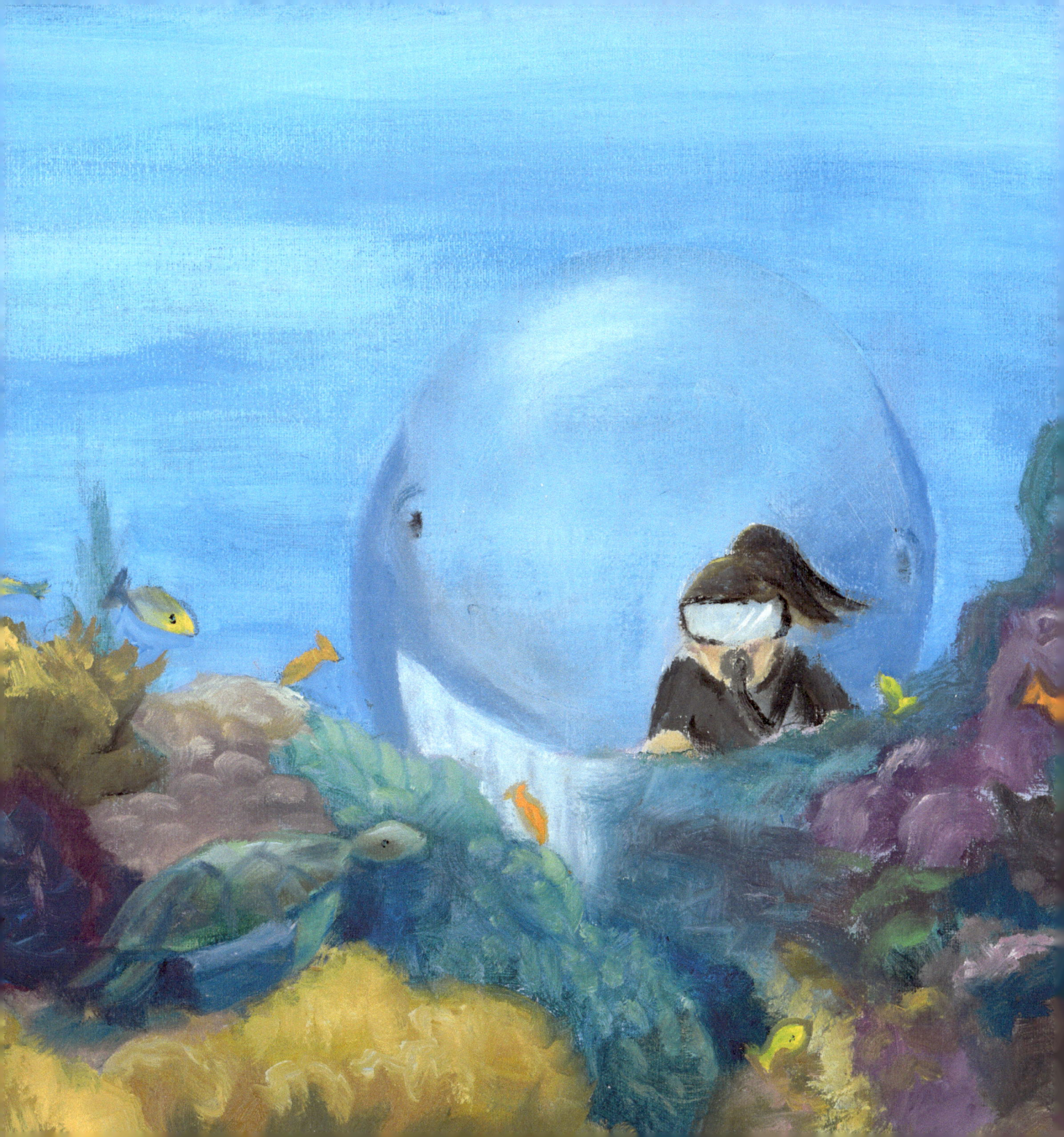

A humpback whale travels a long, long way.
From northern polar waters,
To the tropics, like Hawaii,
True Pacific explorers!

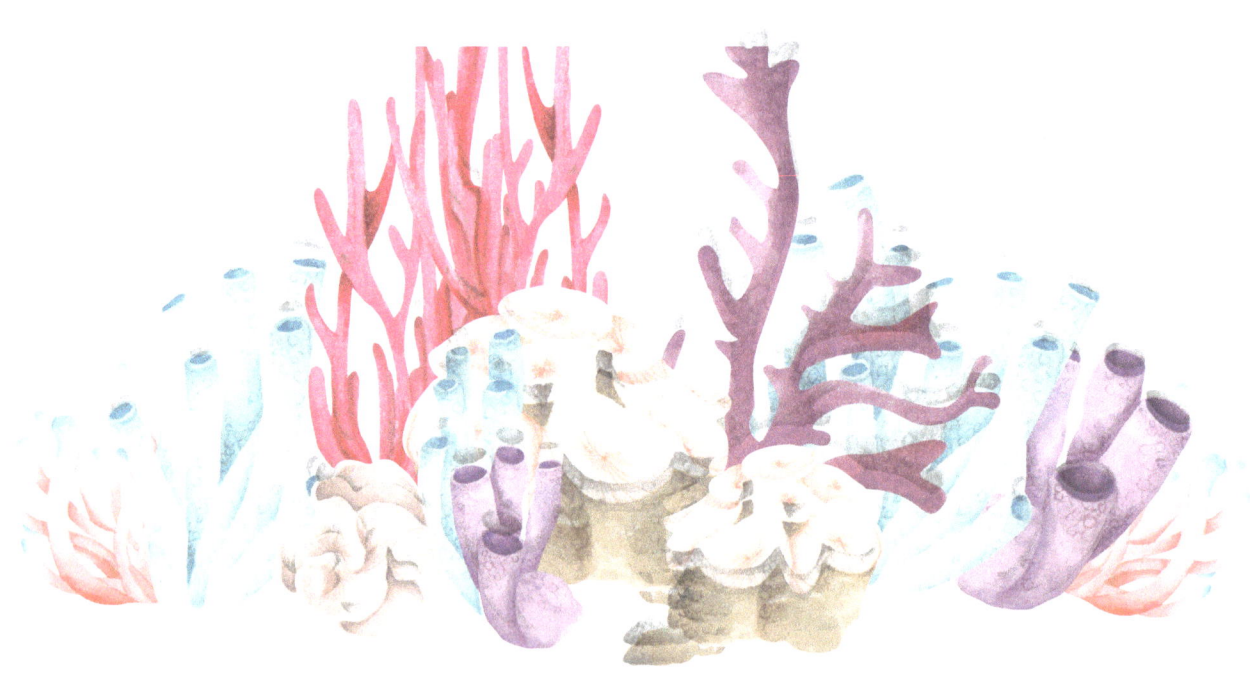

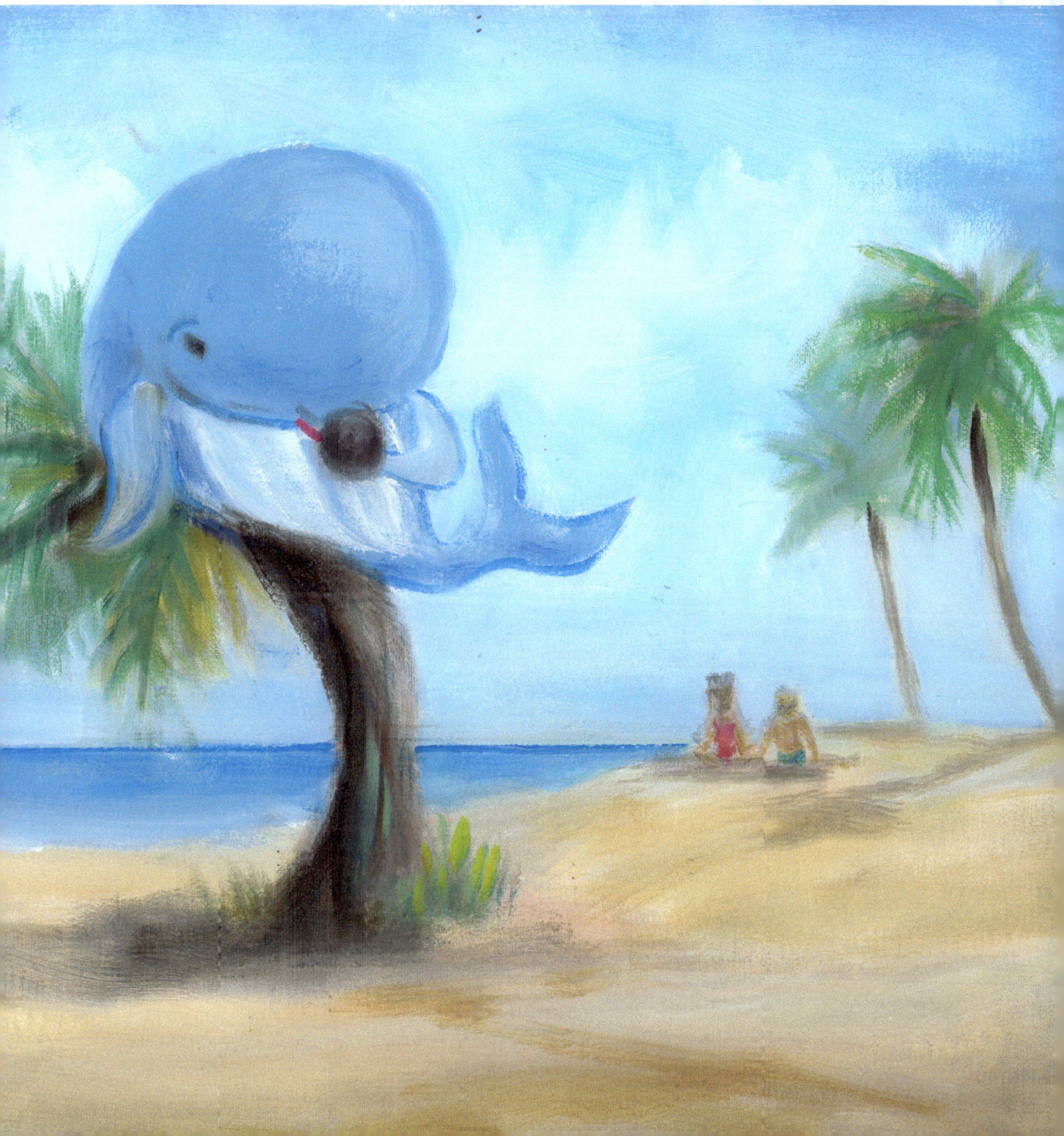

They'll stay in the warmth,
To have their calves,
Then head back to the cold.

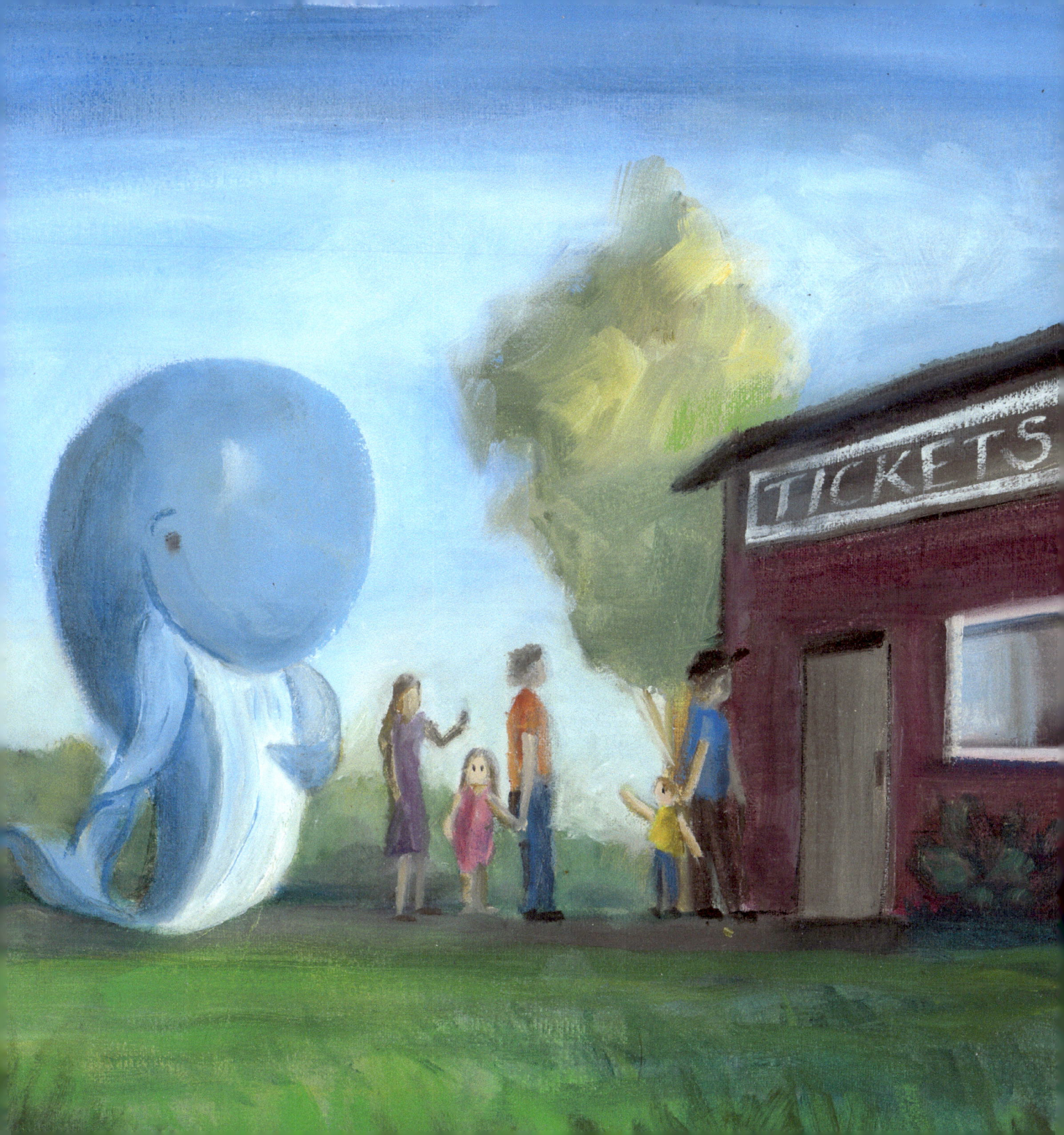

And make this trip many times
'Til they're 80 or 90 years old!

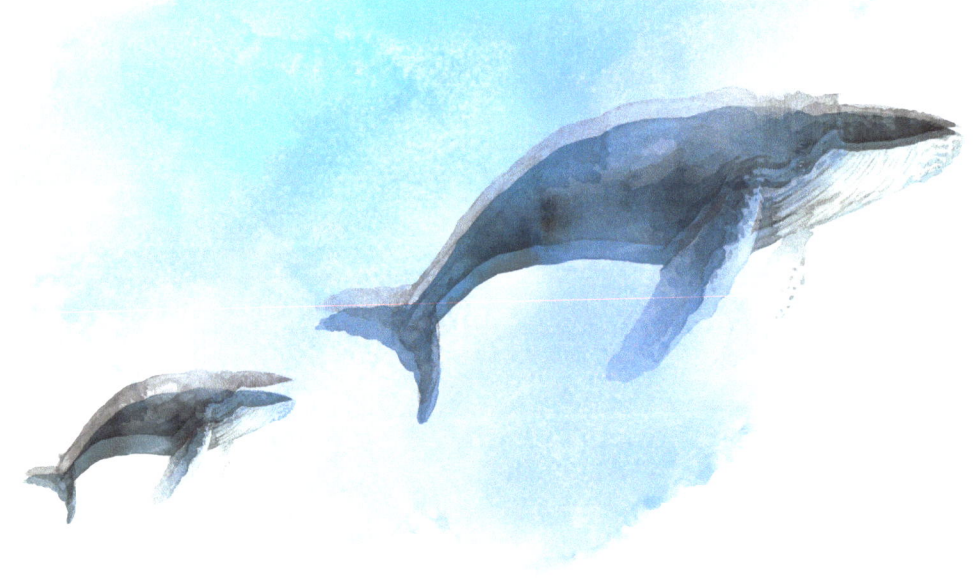

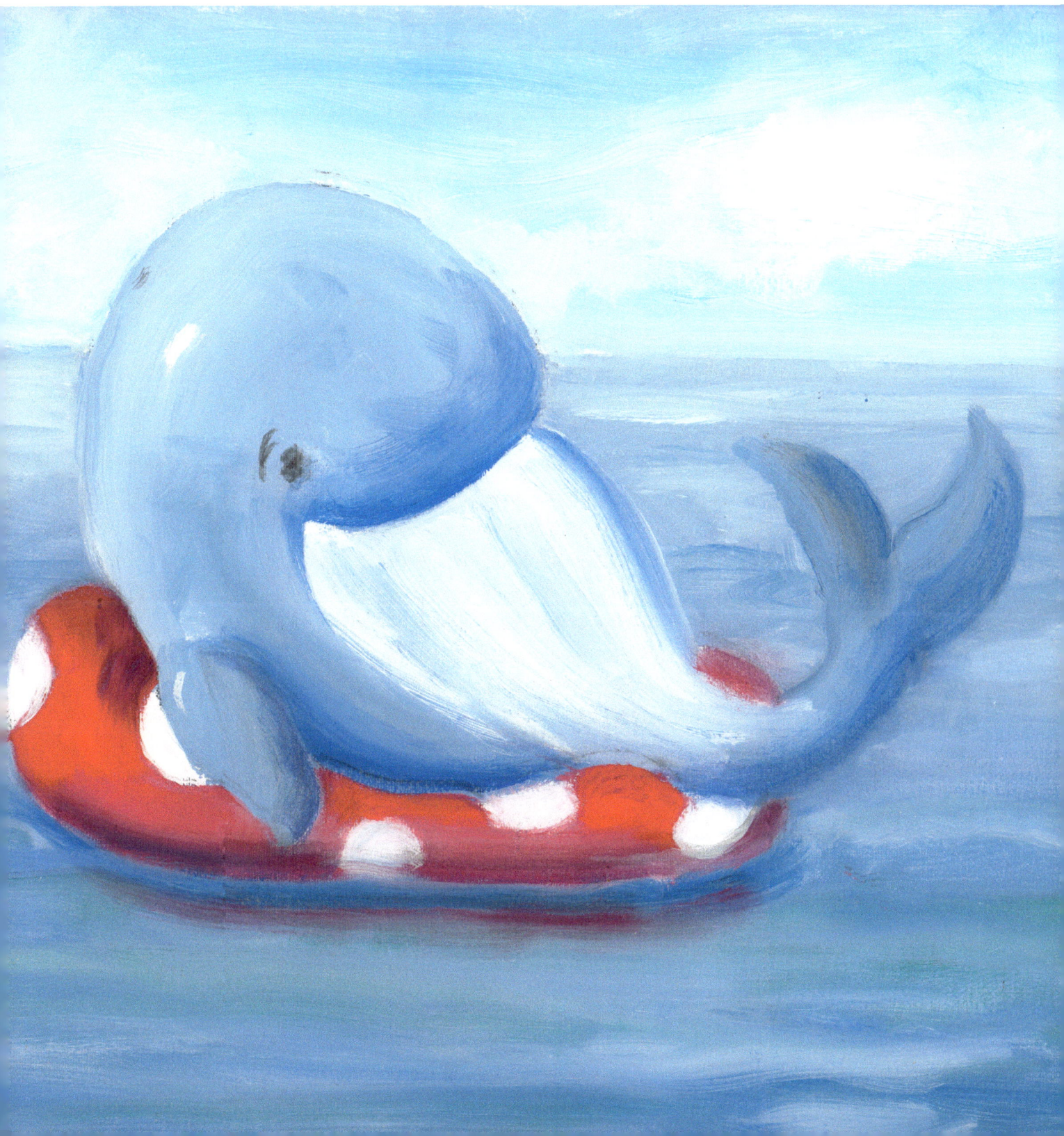

For this kind of journey, they need a lot to eat,
Up to 3,000 pounds per day,
Fish and krill is what they find,
All along the way.

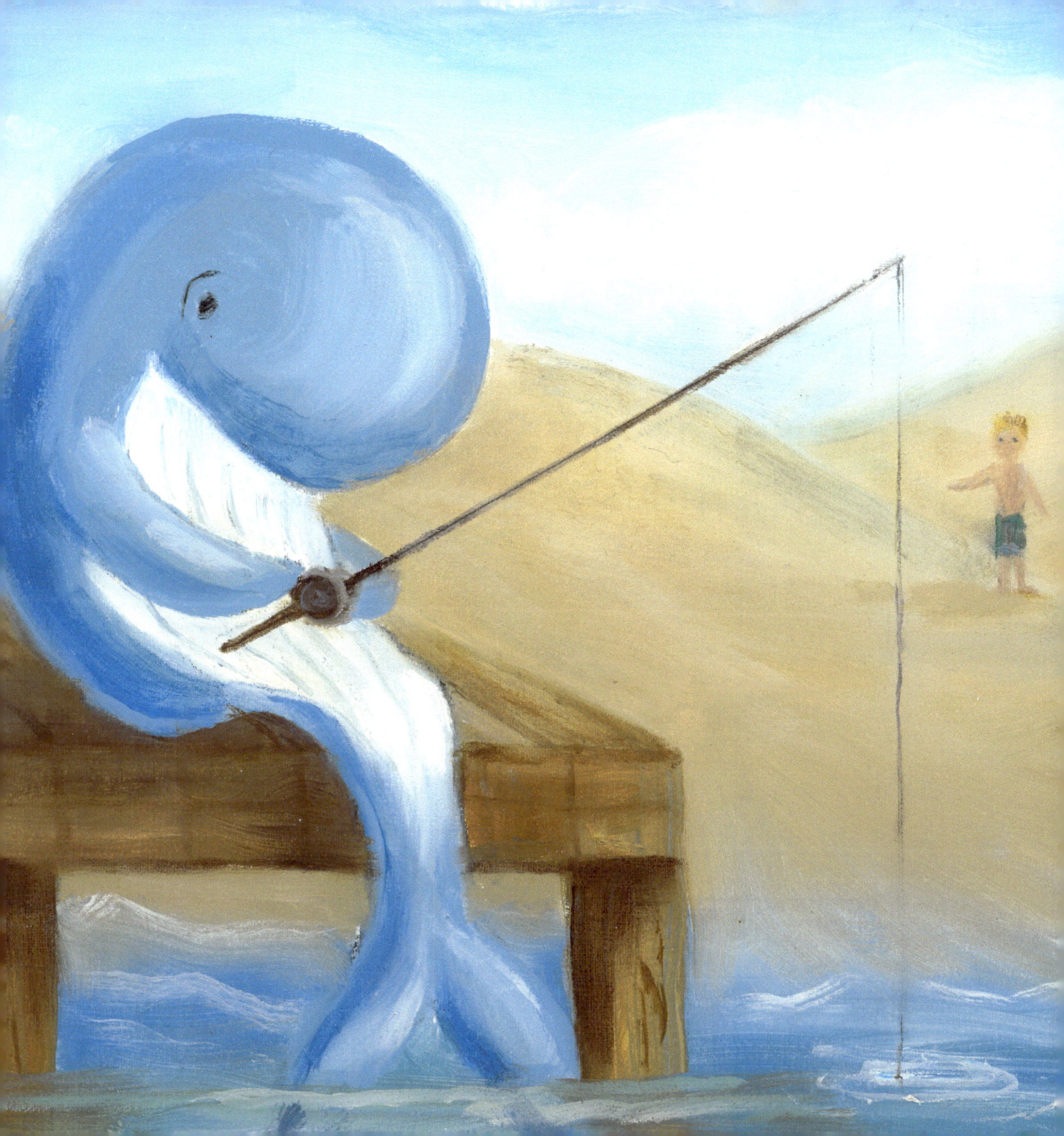

They swim a special path and while
it's fun to watch them go,

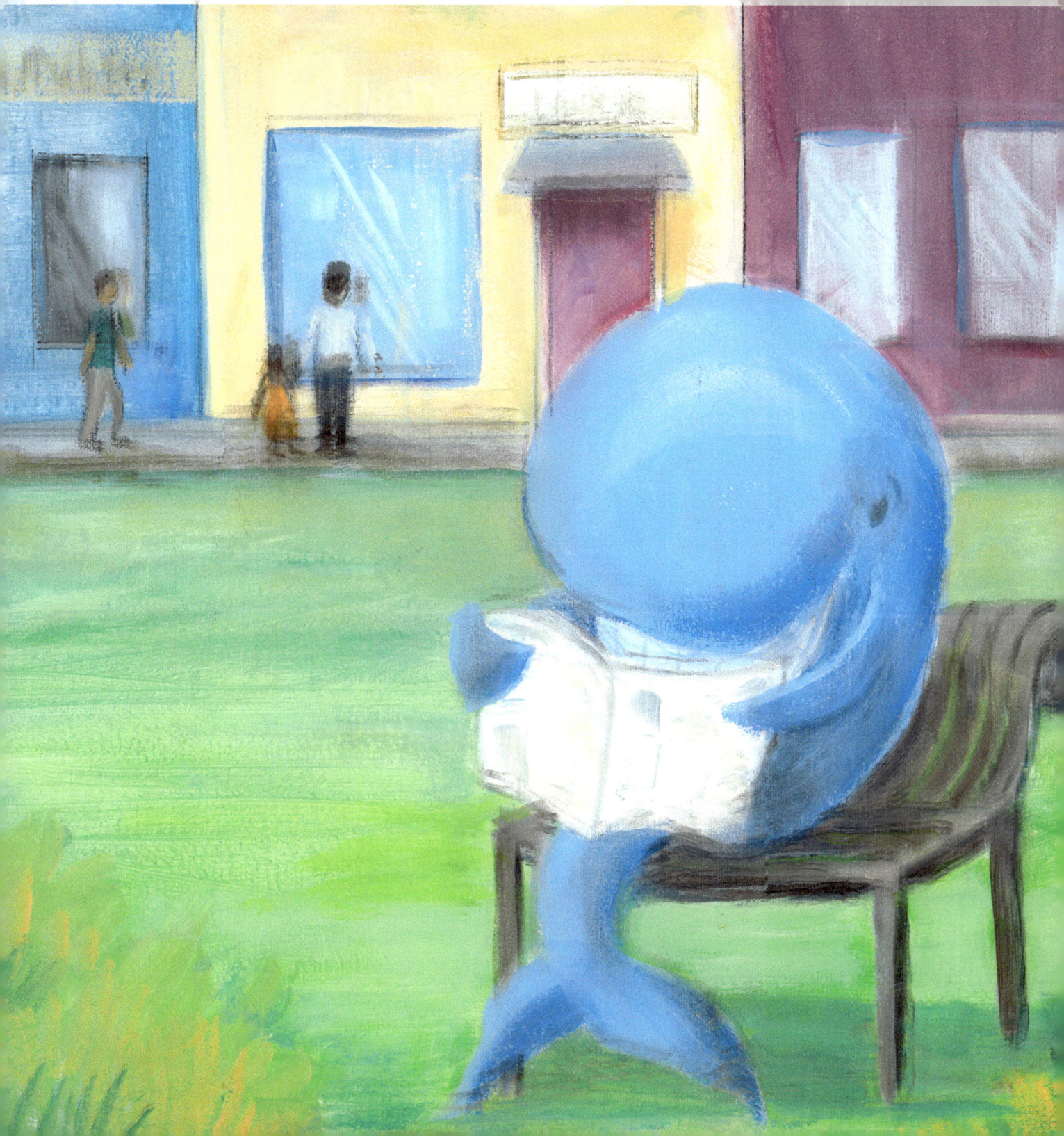

We need to give them space because It's dangerous if boats get too close.

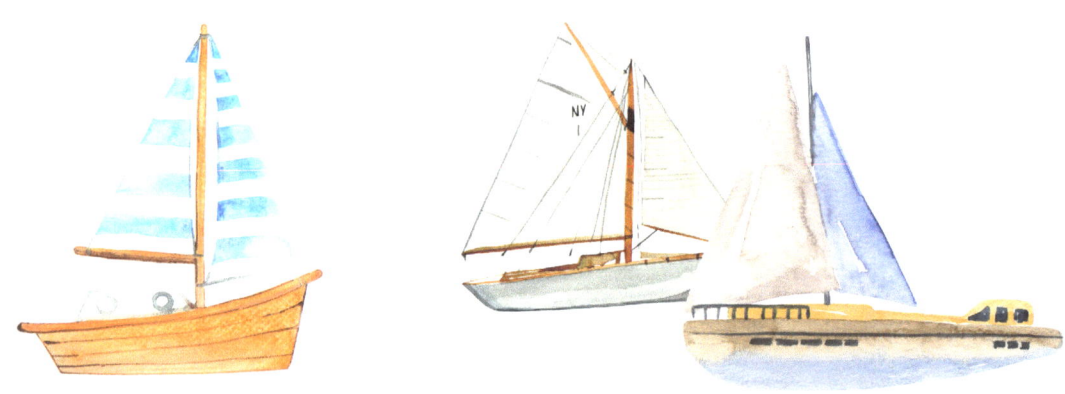

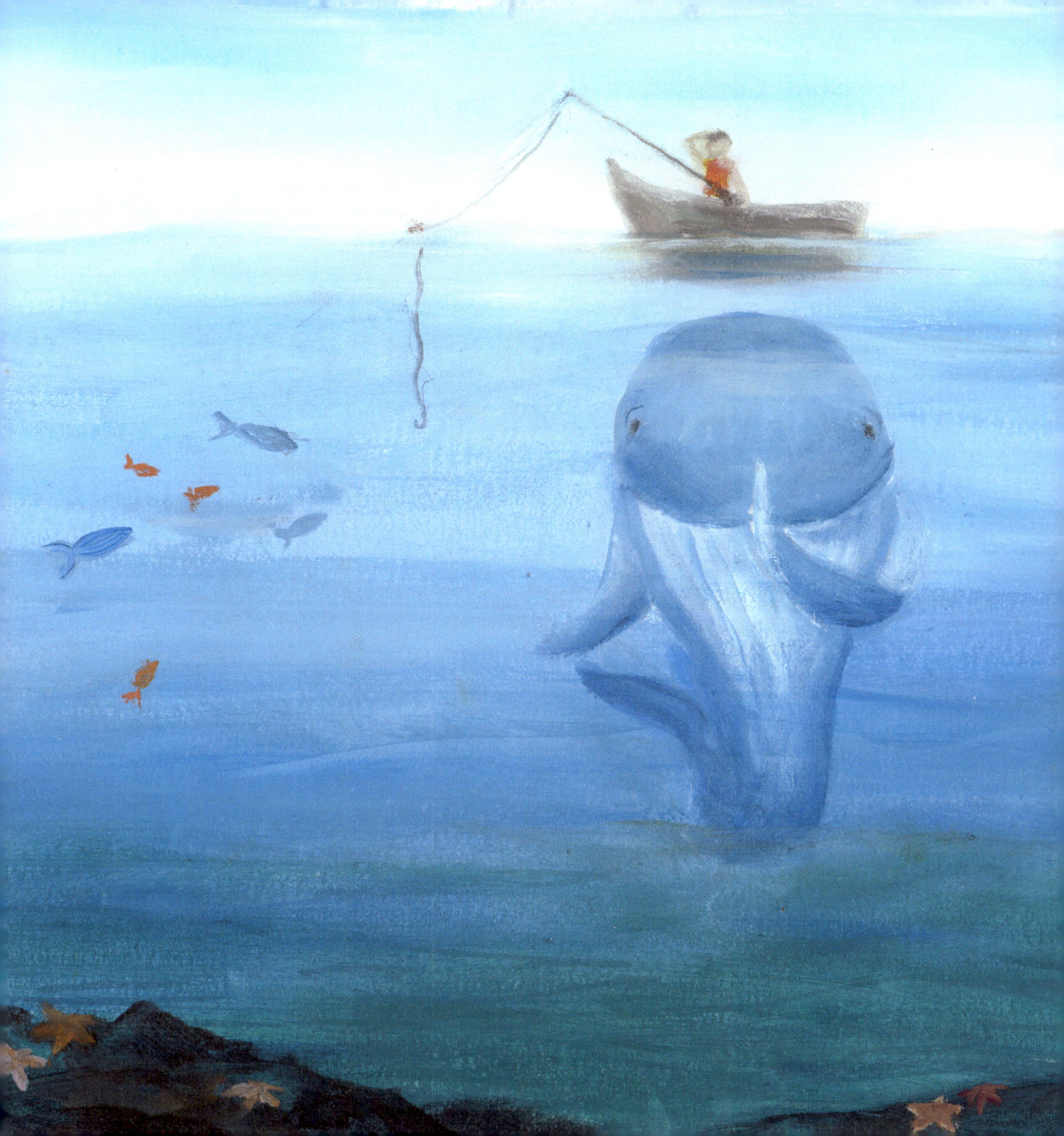

But always keep an eye out
For a whale who may pass by!
You never know where you will spot
Our friendly Whaley guy!

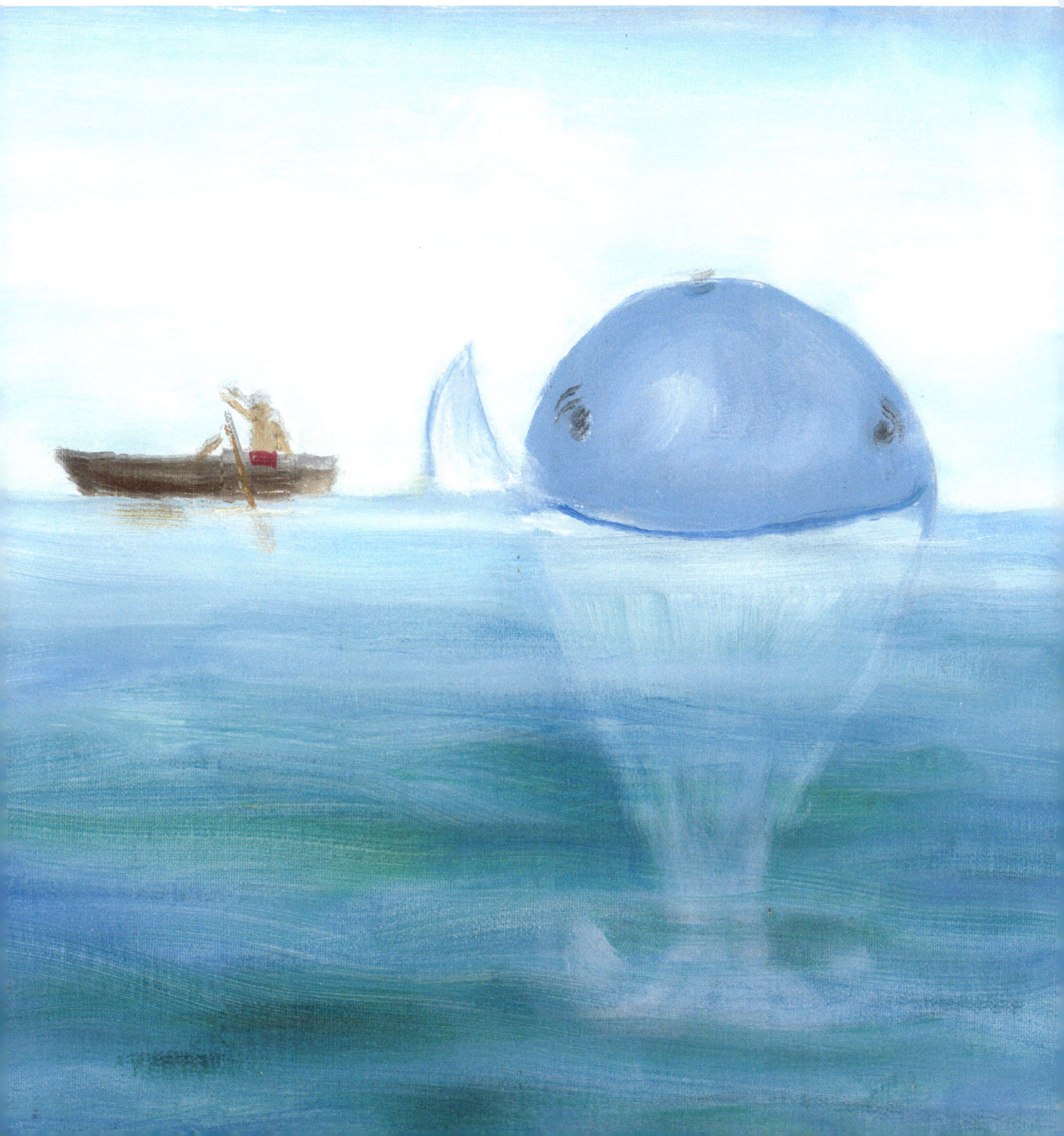

Resources

Navid Nafiue "How Long Do Whales Live?" Oceanfauna.com 2-2-2023. Accessed 12-2-2023

Humpback Whale. Americanoceans.org. Accessed 12-2-2023

Humpback Whale Facts. Whalefacts.org. Accessed 12-2-2023

Oceana.org. Accessed 12-2-2023

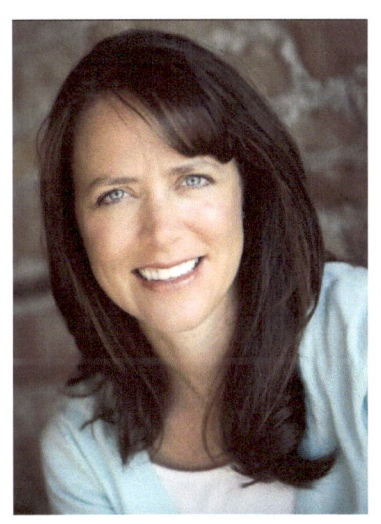

Wendy Jacobs is an author and an artist. Wendy graduated from Brigham Young University with a degree in English and has studied oil painting for more than 30 years. She and her husband live in Utah and count their 6 children and 3 grandchildren as their most precious treasures.

www.ingramcontent.com/pod-product-compliance
Lightning Source LLC
Chambersburg PA
CBHW051941210526
45473CB00006B/2336